I0459730

# A History of Hand Thrown Walls

Adele Evershed

A History Of Hand Thrown Walls
Copyright © 2025 Adele Evershed
Published by Unsolicited Press
Printed in the United States of America
First Edition

All rights reserved. No part of this book may be reproduced or transmitted in any form or by any means, electronic or mechanical, including photocopying, recording, or by any information storage and retrieval system without the written permission of the author, except where permitted by law.

This is a work of fiction. Any resemblance to actual events or persons, living or dead, is entirely coincidental.

Attention schools, libraries, and business: this title can be ordered through Ingram. For special sales, email sales@unsolicitedpress.com.

For information, contact:
Unsolicited Press
Portland, Oregon
www.unsolicitedpress.com
orders@unsolicitedpress.com
619-354-8005

Cover Design: Kathryn Gerhardt
Editor: Summer Stewart

ISBN: 978-1-963115-56-7

Before I built a wall I'd ask to know
What I was walling in or walling out
*Mending Walls-Robert Frost*

# CONTENTS

For my mother, Angela, the one who first believed.

# STONE STEPS

Under the canopy of the grizzled trees, I bend the saplings towards each other, so they look like the gossiping heads of all the Little People guarding the shore of the long river. Then, tying them tightly, we cover them with the tree bark and cut a hole for the fire. Around us, shelters pop up like summer berries. We will do well here; the ground is rich, and our backs are young.

Soon we will start turning the soil. I line up the tools, the sticks, clamshells, and the shells of horseshoe crabs. Through the splotched trunks of the trees, I can see the sacrifice stone; it stands aloof, narrow at the base, and then opening up like a pair of hands cupped shallowly together to receive the offerings of rocks and wood. I have placed a notched white stone I found on the lap of the teeming river as an offering for Konchi Manto, the Great Spirit; in the hope he will bless us with his bounty. The sharp edge of the stone reminds me there is much work to do to prepare for the hard season.

The smells from the cooking pot bring water to my mouth, and my stomach rumbles like the tree frogs mating in the stream. I sit and eat and Seeing Eagle's story about the strange white ghosts floating in long boats to our land is forgotten as I enjoy the golden corn. The cicadas are making music in the trees and my restless mind stills.

When I was a boy, I helped build the serpent walls that undulate through our forest; their dark bodies point the way to water and comfort us as we move. We followed one to this ground;

its snakehead seemed to smile as we struck our camp. Last fall I found few deer and moose, and I had to set snares to catch raccoons, squirrels, or beavers. But here, we can fish and feast on salmon, walleye, and cod. I break off the soft walnut bread and give thanks to the Great Spirit we have endured like the stones. I am the land; it is part of my being like the birds and the beasts, the insects and the fish, each beautiful and strange. My heart will be buried here living within nature to sustain my grandchildren and their grandchildren until the sun no longer blesses these stones.

# THE WISDOM OF THE WHIP-POOR-WILLS

At the edge of the world, the white man banned high voices. It came as no surprise; they always preferred to start arguments in empty rooms knowing this was the only way they could win. When the tribes grumbled, and their grumbles grew legs to take them beyond our rocky borders, the white man started collecting tongues. They buried them in meadows, promising now only the grass would remember the songs. They had forgotten, the grass is made of green blades, and it might cover all the spoilt places, but it can whisper songs of rebellion when the wind moves it.

I sit in the pasture using a blade to tattoo my face with my snake mother's wisdom. I chant an elegy to the breeze about how she puffed silk cut smoke from her nose. When I was little, she wrapped me in ancient threads the color of spring grass, and I traced the flying bird on the belt she always wore. She told me it was her magic girdle, and it held the secret language of women, songs of survival, and hard-won knowledge. She touched each bead and stone, a strange braille, and sang me to sleep, so I drifted away on tales of women healers and recipes to summon the help of the Little People, the kindly spirits that taught us how to grow corn and use healing plants. They keep the earth well and grant favors for those who honor their ways. The red stone eye of the eagle in her girdle glowed, pulsing in the dark wigwam, and it syncopated with the humming in my bones. The stone could make the night seem like the day, and the belt was passed down from mother to daughter as a talisman against injury.

We lived in the high chinks of Moshup's Rock, named for the giant who in his temper threw the rocks that litter our land. Alongside us lived the tarnished walleye, their spotty yellow backs mirrored in the dyed feather dangling from my mother's doughy lobes. It took slow seasons for us to hear the screaking of the white man, yet when it woke my father and brothers, they painted their faces black and yellow to show they were willing to fight to the death. They left, and white men as large as Moshup's ghost killed many women and children, screaming they were taking vengeance upon the heathen. One captured Mother and I and took us to live on his settlement. He would not let us daub our face in white to mourn our men, calling it a pagan ritual—it was a double wound. This man with a ragged mark upon his face the others called Reverend, insisted the word of his God declared women and children should sometimes perish and it was a meritorious deed to teach the savages to live as human beings. He named their settlement a New Canaan and said they were the chosen people.

He also would not let Mother and I sing our songs to the bread to make it soft, so quickly the food we made for our capturer was flat and hard like him. Then, of course, he complained, so my mother hummed quietly before sliding the loaves into the clay oven, but we both knew it would only help a little. Then, he chipped a tooth on his walnut breakfast bread, and his red words left brands on my mother's skin. I implored him to let us sing again, but he threatened to cut out my tongue if I dared even speak, banishing me to a silent breaking.

That night my mother wrapped herself in a sooty cape and crept to the banks of the river. She trilled to bring the fish and begged them to save my voice. She asked them to hide me with the mottled Whip-poor-wills, so I could feast on nectar and learn how to build a nest from cobwebs and bark. I would call 'quirt' in ringing notes to drive away predators and live unafraid to show my black and white bibbed throat. But the fish were always mean and bony specimens that liked to drive a hard bargain. My mother had to barter her girdle to warm their spindly bodies before they would hold me in their mouths and swim away. They left her naked and unprotected. Her last kindness was to smother our jailor so he could not hunt me down; she shaped him into red garnets and scattered them over our home, the place the white man now calls The Devil's Footprint.

I stayed with the birds learning to gather cobwebs, pollinate plants and look in at doors. I sharpened my beak on the white-notched stone I found in the forest. But I could still hear the humming of my mother and her mother before her; it buoyed a boat hidden in my bones. I regrew my legs and floated off to sit in the long grass.

I have gathered all the songs, and it is time for me to raise my voice and smash things. Around my neck, I have hung an amulet of bright red stone so it will be close to my throat as I sing. Listen in the bright dawn, and you will hear tender violence, the noise of women. And you will know that a song can make you a revolutionary or a coward. The choice was always yours.


### A Letter From Utopia

*My Dearest Beth,*

*How I miss your quiet counsel and our walks after church. Life is so very different in this new world. I trust you received my previous letters? I am still waiting on word from you but hope that the next ship will bring the comfort of your words every day. I have written before of our new Reverend. How fortunate we think ourselves for being blessed with a man whose oratory burns with the light of God. The Reverend*

Timms was a true believer, but I'm sure you'll forgive me for writing this—his words could be a little dull. What with this and the long journey to Norwalk for services, I would find myself daydreaming—smiling about when we were girls telling charmed tales in the meadow behind our farm until Father's sharp glance would bring me back into my body.

I must recount Reverend Cooperman's sermon, the one he delivered this Sunday past on the grassy tump, raised as if by the word of God. Our new Meetinghouse is to be constructed around this mound as it is the very centre of our settlement. He called his sermon grandly, 'The Making Of Utopia.' It was dusk and the sky a pretty pink hue. I shivered I do swear when I heard the throaty call of a Whip-poor-will. They are the brown-grey birds so plentiful here, and they get their name for the sound they make. I would not call it bird song, for tis more melancholic, ~~like a girl pining for her love~~. I scratched that last, knowing Father would disapprove. But it was no match for the thundering voice of our Reverend. I asked him for his writings so I might copy them into this letter. I wanted to make sure I had everything perfect so you could feel the power of his words. He very graciously lent me his writings and even offered me ink if I was lacking. Unlike many men, Father has always encouraged my learning and taught me my letters, as you know. I have fond memories of us scratching our names in the mud together. Father thinks it even more important for a woman to read the word of God now so we can help grow His Christian charity in this strange place.

So here is the sermon, in total-

"And I say unto you the English are the Israelites banished to a narrow land. It has been preordained in the eternal struggle against the Devil and his minions that this land will be ours. Those who would drape their darkened bodies in the skins of animals to keep out the cold or run naked in the warming breezes show no shame. This land is *teeming with timber and stones, yet they shun building permanent shelter. They do not farm the land but for some poor patches of woebegone corn or even keep cattle, preferring to hunt down beasts. Is that not contrary to the laws of nature? The exploitation of the land for the profit of man being God's plan. As it was written in Joshua 17:14, "You are numerous and very powerful. You will have not only one allotment but the forested hill country as well. Clear it, and its farthest limits will be yours." So we will cast out these idolatrizing Canaanites by righteous violence, and our presence will be like a city on a hill, a beacon to all who follow the word of God."*

*His words have always secretly warmed my belly, and I look forward to Sundays now as I used to look forward to the days we had plum duff for pudding. In truth, I did quibble with myself when we first arrived as to whether God meant us to take the lives of the Indians. Surely it would be better to convert them and grow His flock? However, when I voiced my misgivings to Father, he did remind me that the Indians are descendants of Ham. He took down our family Bible and turned to the Book of Genesis; his voice is gruff, and he does not imbue the words with holy light as does the Reverend, but it did vibrate with conviction when he spoke from rote about the banishment of Ham for mocking his father, Noah, and how he taught his children to worship the Devil. Still, it was only when the native women that Reverend Timms had rescued fled in the night, leaving in their wake bloody drops as large as stones did I feel the Indians were no better than animals. In truth, they are worse because animals have to kill to survive. Reverend Timms had bestowed nothing but Christian kindness, and they killed him anyway.*

*On to something brighter. Do you remember I wrote about Luke Symonds? We met aboard The Arbella. Well, dearest one, he is planning to ask Father that we be married. He gave me an unusual keepsake, a white stone shaped like a heart. He had drilled a hole and threaded a lace through so I could fasten it. So just think the next time*

15

*I write, I might be Mistress Symonds. I only wish your presence here to complete my happiness.*

*Your loving friend,*

*Abigail*

*I just heard a Whip-poor-will outside—a good omen. I will try to spy it on my way to return Reverend Cooperman's writings.*

Beth, I have enclosed the letter my dearest Abigail left unsealed in her room. I am so sorry to impart that she disappeared the same day she wrote these words to you. Abigail's betrothed found her necklace on a low stonewall of one of the farms here but of Abigail there was no sign. Although others have told me I should abandon hope, I will not. They fill my ears with horrors about bears or worse. Please keep Abigail in your prayers my dear, with God's grace we will find her soon.

# THE WAILING STONE

The cracks in my hand match the fissures in the wall; they tell our stories better than any words ever could. The sun is high and bright; it has warmed the stones, so they pulse as if they are alive. Each one I stack screams like the rat I watched giving birth in the barn last night. I was so fascinated by the violence of it, the slimy pink bodies popping out onto the dirty straw as the mother's pink eyes wept bloody streaks that I didn't hear my father's worn boots coming over the cobbles. Pushing me aside, so I fell onto the ground; he hit the mother and babies with a large rock, leaving me to mop up the pulpy mess. I wonder if that killing stone is one he is placing now as rubble between the two laid walls to allow everything to settle.

Since arriving in Connecticut, it seems all we've farmed is stone; the land is littered with them, some as large as houses. When I was a young boy, my mother told me tales from the old country about the wailing stones that called out to travelers who had lost their way. They told them to lay down their burdens, stop and rest awhile. Everyone who lay down never got up again. The clasping arms of the wall held them until they too turned grey and hard and in that way the wall grew. Mother always said I should treat the stones we pull up kindly, as each stone has a sad tale to tell. So each time I visit her grave, I leave a special rock I have found to keep her company. Last Sunday I placed a small white stone, it was shaped like a heart and I had found it at the furthest point of our property. I was so intent on polishing it I never noticed the shadows stealing the fields away. As I stumbled home I realized I'd be going to bed hungry. My father does not believe in making accommodations for latecomers and I knew my supper would already be in the dog's belly. As I put the stone on Mother's grave I imagined it telling her I missed her with my whole heart.

An unseen choir of frogs is rumbling deep in the woods, their song sounds like a reprimand. Maybe they are angry with us for taking the land for pasturing from the natives. There are but a handful of that old tribe here, miserably destitute, the rest having left or died off. I feel no amount of praying at the meetinghouse can take away this sin. I place a stone shaped like an anvil, its top curves slightly inward and I wonder if I will find its match.

I stop to wipe my face, take my shirt off and listen to the discordant noise of the frogs. I take paper and pencil from my pocket and scratch some words.

*I woke up yellow—decrepit—something not quite right*
*People born of the stones are older—yet this weathering surprised me*

*The compression of the thing settled in my gut*
*Rigmaroling me round like a drunk—yet I still couldn't fill up the empty spaces*

*Time once felt slippery in patches—skidding past—a flibberty-jibbit*
*Now it just hangs like a promise—each day a small fable*

*I dig out abeyant words—yet use them in all the wrong places*
*Washing them with my breath—so they can exist for a short time*

*Capering about they create their own mild breeze*

*—amorphous*

*—they float away on a riptide and I am too gutless to call them back*


I have been working on this poem for a while and feel a sense of satisfaction that I have managed to finish it. It might be my best one yet. I cannot tell father but the *Hartford Courant* has agreed to publish one of my poems, My Heart is a Notched Stone. It will appear next week and might be the beginning of a whole new life.

Father appears as if he's been summoned by my lack of industry and I have no time to stuff my paper into the crevice of the wall where I have hidden my other poor attempts at poetry. "Why have you stopped? You'd better not be writing those nonsense verses of yours. I swear over my dead body I will not let poetry harden you into devilry," he says gruffly. Around us, the day laborers pick up the pace of their work. If he looks, he will see they are piling the wall carelessly, and stones will be lost before too long. We will have to rebuild to stop our sheep breaching them. But he only has eyes for me. He snatches away the sheet, I try to grab it back, and he shoves me. My head strikes the stone with the force of a hammer.

# MELTED MAJESTY

*My Dear Mr. Green,*

*May I first congratulate you on your immense achievement. The publication of 'The Hartford Courant' acknowledges we are no longer some colonial backwater, which can be ignored by the powers that be. I am sure you agree we must stir the very marrow of the populace and to that end I have penned some humble words of my own. If you see fit you might print them in your next pamphlet.*

*Yours truly,*

*John Trumbell, Hartford, Connecticut July 1774*

**Becoming An Unbeliever**

*White birds glide against a midnight ruffled sky*
*And so my heart a stone, white and notched*
*My liver and spleen—pebbles*
*I burn and melt majesty into bullets*

*And taxation is a tinker's dam that I shall no longer build*
*Nor heed the velvet choker of rich mercy*
*That great untruth told to keep peaty men tamped down*
*Ankle deep in the muddy gutters of the world*
*That speaks of reaching God's acre hoisted on gossamer and incense*
*To gaudy Elysium*

*But I think more likely than not*
*That once we climb that steepled slope to dreamland*
*We will glimpse through the mizzle—*
*Our Lords*
*Still Kings in this heavenly domain*
*As once below they ruled*
*Troubled not by our consumptive rattling*
*Though we make the twelve gates tremble*
*For all that—we will be spackled with pearly wisdom*
*An eternity of better tomorrows vowed to all*
*Once we slay the ravens that disturb their forever home*

*We who live this knickknack life—the make do and mend people*
*Steeped in bone broth memory of unfed times*
*And brittle hardtack living*
*And too often feel the swarthy hand of fate's fickle draft*
*They tell us—*
*It is we who must heed the King's men*
*Their wordsmithery honed and hammered smooth,*
*England would have us believe for our obedience*
*We will be called to serve as celestial knights of the Lord*
*Our souls a droplet returned to God's eye*
*Exalted to a blessed life of milk and honey*

*But listen not*
*Uncommon feats*
*Will never raise the common man*
*In this life or the next*

*You may sift us to fine dust*
*But one day we will rouse*
*The tremolo of our living banished*
*And in its stead a crescendo*
*Breaking over the quaggy bogs*
*The walking almost dead*
*Afeared no longer*
*Singing out as one*
*"We are the unbelievers and you should run"*

# THE OVALS

*Run away from the subscriber on the night of the 4th of May, a Black girl about fifteen years of age named Hannah, formerly the property of the undersigned. She is cunning and artful, which has caused her to be much whipped, and thus, you will know her by the scars on her back. She is also missing the small finger on her left hand. When she went away, she stole sundry Clothes and about 3 Pounds Cash. I will give 40s if she is taken and delivered back to me in Maryland.*

<u>Maryland Gazette John Trueheart, 8th of June 1846</u>

My daughter's eyes were like melting pools of ice as she handed the runaway slave advertisement to me, and I knew I must move my passenger sooner than I had planned.

When Hannah arrived, the signs of her mistreatment were not just written on her body; they were carved in her mind. Her night terrors so strong I thanked the Lord once more for the remoteness of our farm. I had hoped for more time to settle her before the next stage of the journey, but there are people hereabouts who would sell their grandmother for a porcelain pot, so I cannot afford to tarry any longer.

The next station is my brother's house in Wilton, Connecticut, and from there, she will travel to the Grand Central Station at Farmington. In case of a raid, my brother William dug a tunnel, but the ground here does not allow any such recourse. He wrote a letter complaining about the stones he was finding as he constructed the passage, he said they were 'sprinkled like curses.' He called his house The Ovals after two massive boulders that flank the path and he uses the small white pebbles he raked up as tickets for the underground railway. I have given Hannah one such stone to allow her to board. She stared at it bright in her crosshatched palm and murmured her thanks. Then she added that it looked like her heart when she was kept a slave, a piece always missing. She looked so forlorn; rubbing the nub of her missing finger it strengthened my resolve to fight the evils of slavery with every fiber of my being.

When I looked at my daughter, her eyes were ablaze. My gentle Gertrude looked like she would shoot any man who threatened to enslave the poor girl again. She told Hannah that she would find the missing piece of herself now because she was free. And I pray that this will be so.

# THE PALACE THEATER WATERBURY CONNECTICUT IS PROUD TO PRESENT WAR IN FOUR ONE-ACT PLAYS

## Act One: No Such Thing as A Civil War (1865)

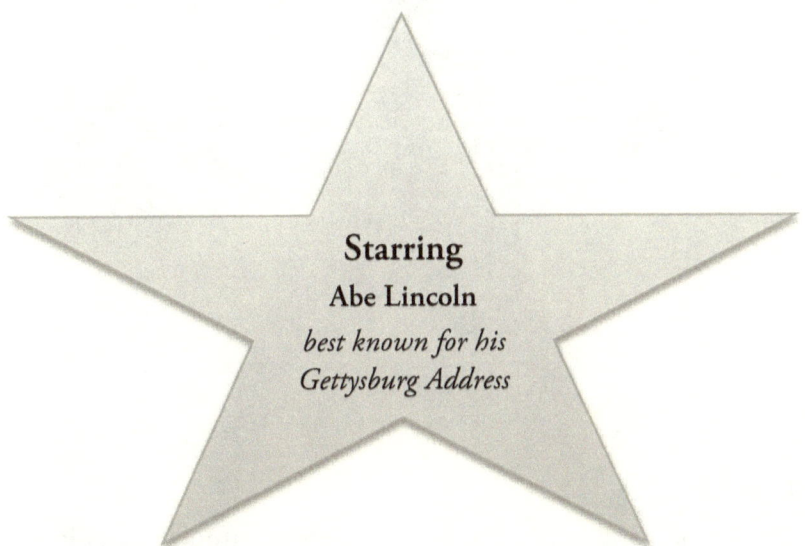

**Starring**
Abe Lincoln
*best known for his
Gettysburg Address*

We remember the hoary men of the North. And the unripe women of every valley who were the keepers of the sublime lie, as the hobbledehoy youth passed by. Dough boys shaped by Mama's hand, looking to make America a shining beacon on a hill. Unsheltered juggins from Wilton or Norwalk or the back of beyond enchanted by empty promises of glory and home by Christmas. Flocking onto ferries, rattling onto carts, walking in the ruts where others had gone before and jumping over stonewalls like racehorses ready to win at all costs. They followed bespoke orders from their betters frayed before they were even worn and then rent ragged ahead of the first forced march south.

## Act Two: A Monologue
## Letter From France (1918)

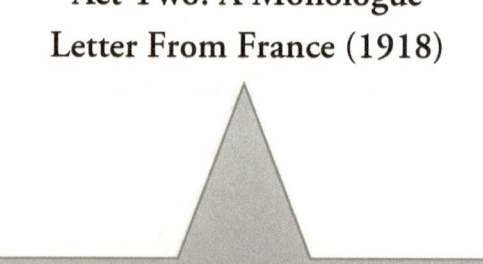

With
Woodrow
Wilson

Dear Mom,

It's all gone to pot. I want to unpack my troubles, sit by the Sound and make salt. Or else climb Bear Mountain to fill my stewed lungs with honeysuckle air, picking up stones to lob into the air to scare the squirrels. Yet we wait. Hushed. Jam-packed like meatballs, steeped in the gravy of tears; heart, liver, and belly, churning. Jesus Mom, to forget for just a minute now. But I am blistered by remembrances, lashed to the 'Last Post,' under this perishing sky. Wearisome am I of the chunder and caterwaul; the septic stench of the maybe scent of lilacs. This muck of war is an oil slick on the souls of men and we will never scrub it off. No, not even in a hundred years.

Your Loving Son

Franklin

## Intermission—brought to you by 'Connecticut Magic Rocks' and The Rock-Ettes

*Heal what ails you with our rocks, our rocks,*

*Heat them up and put them in your smelly socks,*

*Grind them up and you can drink them*

*Stop the flu or gout or phlegm*

*With our rocks, our rocks, our rocks.*

**Straight from the Constitution State to improve your constitution or your money back!! Especially effective in preventing Spanish flu.**

# Act Three: Encore

And
Franklin
Delano
Roosevelt

The audiences take their seats—primed to cheer. This revival has stellar reviews from papers and politicians alike. But something seems skew-whiff; last year's blood-rusted cast litters the stage both hero and pantomime villain alike awash in lime. The audience fidgets—bring on the understudies. So new actors debut-no time for rehearsal, their moves already blocked and headlines set, "Allies Smash Germany On The Beaches." No matter that their marshmallow toes stick and sink sodden in the boggy treads.

They receive a standing ovation from the lardy crowd relishing another happy ending.

The clapping like gunshot rings in their ears as they stumble blindly into the wings.

This was the finest show yet—Encore-Encore!

## Act Four: At the Cenotaph

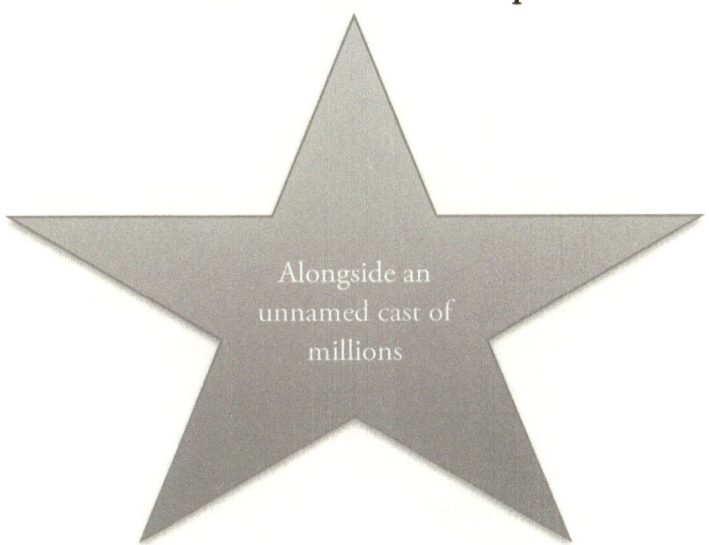

Alongside an unnamed cast of millions

And for each name recorded on a list their mother, wife, sweetheart, daughter, place a notched heart as a rock in remembrance—and each Memorial Day we all take the cold comfort of words chiseled in stone.

Don't fret if you can't make this performance, there is sure to be a revival with new material and new cast members soon!

# JUST THE TONIC

*My Babbles has a nasty knack of keeping a monkey on her back and in her bed.* I looked at what I had written. My Babbles was no longer in the present tense, but I couldn't bring myself to kill her off on the page as I had in real life. I picked up my pen and started again.

*After my mother died, my Aunty Barbara took me in. Each night she cocooned me in a blanket that smelt of lily-of-the-valley and cigarettes and told me stories of Ashbury, the house where she and my mother had grown up. She took me to the theatre, even to plays others thought unsuitable for a young girl, like "War in Four Acts" at The Palace Theatre.*

This seemed like a better start; I picked up the stone I had found out walking in Devil's Den. I conjured my aunt in my mind's eye. She was a curvy woman who favored a low pompadour, so her hair rose in regimented curls, each with a steely golden glint. Then, in my head, I heard her say, "Tell him one of the ghost stories I told you about Ashbury that could fill a book, never mind a page." I shook my head and spoke out loud, my voice soft from lack of use, "No, Babbles, Dr. Gordon wants to know what you were like and why I killed you."

Sighing, I put a line through everything I had written. None of it gave a picture of my Babbles. I looked again at the first sentence. I knew it was true because I'd heard Babbles tell two of her bridge ladies, "What can I tell you? I like men. They've always been like monkeys on my back." But I was fourteen and didn't know what that meant. That day Fallon Carlyle who usually made up the fourth had sent a message that she was indisposed, so they had let me play even though I played too fast and mismanaged my trumps.

Each Wednesday evening, my aunt would dress in her best silks, loop a rope of pearls around her long neck and waft out of the house surrounded by fragrant clouds of Molinard Habanit she had dropped on her cigarettes. I would always ask where she was going, but she would never say. She had promised she would never lie to me as my mother had about the illness that killed her, so Babbles never pretended she was off to the opera or a dinner party or anything.

On the whole I had a happy life until the incident and now I know I'm unlikely to have a happy hour again. I take a string and thread it through the hole in the small white stone. I tie it around my neck and let it nestle between my breasts so at least I have the illusion of having a heart.

You see, Babbles was having an affair with Henry Fallon. He was the monkey she had kept on her back and in her bed. Their whole circle was aware of the connection apart from Fallon herself. But then one of the papers got hold of a photograph of my aunt and Henry Fallon leaving a hotel in the early hours of the morning, her hair loose down her back. They ran it on the front page.

That day I spent the day in the library, my mind in a spin. My aunt had swept out of the house at midday, only returning in the early evening. I had met her at the door, and she had said, "Virginia, I know you must have questions for me, and I will answer them all. Now go and change. I promise you nothing is so serious to stop us from keeping up appearances."

As I was processing the implications of my aunt's mood, there was a loud knocking at our door. My aunt's voice shouted out, "Fallon, how lovely to see you. You are just in time for cocktail hour do come in." Catching sight of me at the top of the stairs my aunt said, "Virginia please ask Mary to bring some refreshments." Fallon, her voice raised, said, "Barbara, how could you? You will be dead to society." The door of the parlor slammed.

I knew it was Cook's night off as I went into the pantry to retrieve the bottle of strychnine she kept on the top shelf for the rats in our alley. I asked Mary to set up a tray and told her I would take it up myself.

As I entered the room, I saw my aunt had a red welt across her cheek. I set the tray down and kept my back to them as I dropped the poison into the glass and then I poured the gin. Finally, I turned and offered the drink to Fallon Carlyle but she refused, saying, "No thank you Virginia, I'll not be drinking tonight." At that, my aunt took the glass from my trembling hands, saying, "Well, I certainly need a drink."

I think I screamed; I'm told I fainted and hit my head on the edge of a table. My Babbles suffered a most horrible death, and Fallon Carlyle was arrested for her murder after they found the bottle of strychnine under the sofa. I think it must have rolled there when I fell.

I finish writing my confession and add bromide from my prescribed sleeping powder to my medicine. This will cause the strychnine in my tonic to sink to the bottom of the bottle, leaving behind a lethal dose. I clutch the stone heart, it is warm in my palm and I hope they will bury it with me.

# BLACKBERRY WINTER

We all knew Bernie was dead. Papa had even dug a hole next to Johnny's grave beside the low slung wall of stones that bound our small patch on this earth. When he came in, he took off his work boots and told Mama, "Johnny will be a good big brother and look after our baby girl until we all meet in heaven, God willing." Mama didn't say anything; she rocked Bernie in the cradle on the floor and picked up a rag to clean off the clod from his boots as if Papa might need them to go back out to work soon. But Papa's job like Johnny had been gone for a long while now.

The following day Mama peeled herself from her chair and spruced up the house as if we were expecting company. Then she turned her attention to my brothers and me slicking down their hair and saying to me, "May bug git yourself outta those raggedy pants and put on your best polka-dot dress." When none of us moved, she snapped, "Hurry now. Why are you lolling about like a puddle of long sweetening?" Papa took her gently by the shoulders and tried to lead her back to her seat, but she shook him off like a shower of rain.

Mama looked slaunchwise at him and shuddered as if she was breaking from the inside out. And then she unpacked her black dress, the one she kept wrapped in plastic. The rustling made me think of the wren that had flown into our house the week before Bernie passed. Mama had taken the broom to it, stunning it, and as I watched, she hit the wee mottled bird with the cooking pan. I let out a squeal like one of the wild piglets, and Mama turned to me, her eyes like foxfire, and said, "Oh May bug, I needed to git it before it could get word to God." Teacher had declared all these old beliefs just superstitions, but I could see Mama was scared. She believed if a bird flies into the home, someone would die. After my sister, Bernadette, passed, I never put much store by what Teacher said ever again.

Mama stood up straight as if she was addressing the Reverend and said, "I've been a-studying about how to say this till I've nigh wearied myself to death. Mary-Jo told me...." Papa interrupted, tutting, "Now that woman's tongue's a mile long. I put no store by any of her wild tales." Mama continued as if he hadn't spoken, "There's a man taking photos for a New York magazine in the Cove. He's already been to the Mobley's to photograph poor wee Riva. You know she's backset with the measles." Papa stretched his neck as if he had a crick, "I hope you ain't saying that mule trader is hooving himself here?" His voice had deepened, and his eyes were like chips of coal. I could feel the waspers in the air that Papa could let loose when he was vexed and backed against the wall. My brothers, skittish, came to join me. I took my lucky white stone out of my pocket. It was the only thing Papa brought from his home in Bridgeport when he came here to mine coal. His Mama had given it him as a good luck token and told him it was a thank you gift from the family of a girl she had prepared for burial. It is shaped like a heart with a hole in the middle that I can fit my pinkie finger in. It feels rough like the scars on Mama's arms.

But although Mama peaked, she said, "I allowed he'd git here this afternoon." Mama picked up Bernie from the cradle and started to sing a lullaby as she dressed her in the white coat and matching booties she had knitted not a year ago.

This was the only time I ever saw Mama defy Papa, and it not end in a whopping. The man from *Time* magazine came and took our photo. It was a blue cold day when he crossed over Line Fork

Creek on the rickety bridge to our two-room shack, but at least the temperature meant he couldn't smell the sewage frozen in the water. Papa told us all not to smile, said it wouldn't be proper. And he refused to put on his boots or put out his roll-up. When the photographer left Mama pressed the heart stone into his palm as a thank you. He looked at it and seemed about to give it back to her but I think the look in her eye stopped him. He slipped it into one of the pockets of his coat that crackled like bacon when he moved.

Later, Mary-Jo cut out the photo and brought it over for Mama. When Papa saw it, he took the belt to Mama, leaving her with indigo bruises up and down her arm. All that winter, Papa raised welts on Mama; they sprang up like clumps of blackberries on the forest of her body. And like a forest Mama stayed silent, letting the fury pass over her like the wind.

Papa never said why the photo made him so vexed, but I think it was because Mama was smiling, and he knew nothing we could do would ever make her smile again.

# A FISHY TALE

They say we women are invisible, but we're not. We are just overlooked, and well, that's a different thing altogether. Men have always worked at sea, harvesting the fish and the stories. They strode with such big steps and rigged their boats with such clattering it was easy to forget they were the ones who were invisible for days or weeks at a time. But without us, they would have been left like fishes out of water.

God knows we worked hard; my hands looked like they belonged to an old woman, the skin on my fingers crisped and peeling from all the soaking. Sometimes I wished I could turn into a fish myself, I'd let my skin harden into scales, and with a flick of my tail, I would leave my life behind me.

I lived in Haddam, although it has never felt like home. My family always had one hand on the Bible and one on the tiller. You see, fish swam in our bloodstream. The men made their living on the Connecticut River, and the women silently mended the nets and filleted the fish for market. So, I knew this would be my life, from the age of being able to heft a bucket.

When I was young, I was expected to collect the scraps of bone and offal and feed them to Jessie, our pig. She was my only friend; the other children only teased me about my smell. They acted as if they all smelt like lavender soap rather than stale sweat or mildew. I would swish my braid, clutch my lucky stone, and call over my shoulder, "I am a shad princess tasked with spying on your kind for my father the king, and one day, when we know enough about

your wicked ways, he will come and sweep you all into the river."
Then I would run to Jessie's shed and rub my tears on her soft side
as she rumbled sounds of comfort to block out the echo of the
jeering that had trailed behind me. I would take my lucky talisman
out of my pocket and rub my finger in the groove and will my heart
to be as still as the milky stone. I found it on the shore of our river
when I had gone to escape the tempest raging inside our house. It
looked like a charm in the shape of a love heart and the second I
picked it up I felt my own heartbeat slow, Daddy's harsh words
dissolved like blood in salt water, and I knew that one day I would
leave Haddam behind.

As I got older, the other children grew tired of taunting me.
They might hold their noses as I walked past, but they never spoke
to me apart from Jimmy Boulanger. He would approach crab-like,
so I never saw him coming. I would feel his sticky breath on my
neck, and he would pinch me, saying, "Just checking you have skin
and not scales, princess." And then he'd run away laughing. He
followed me from school one day, and as I walked through Bates
Field, he pushed me down. He said, "We all know you smell of
rotting fish because you're a sea witch," and then he lay on top of
me and started breathing heavily; he smelt of vinegar, and as he
covered my mouth with his, I felt like I was sinking into a pickle
barrel. I could feel his tongue knocking on my teeth, so I opened
my mouth wider and then clamped my teeth down on his tongue.
My mouth filled with rust; he screamed and kicked me as I lay on
the ground, and it all felt like it had happened to me before.

I thought I might tell my mother, have her stroke my hair,
and tell me it would all be okay. But when I looked at her eyes,
they had sunk so far into her face she looked as if she was not really
there. So, instead, I decided to start carrying my filleting knife with
me from then on.

The next time Jimmy Boulanger looked at me, I took my knife out of my pocket and ran it over my thumb. His eyes widened as I smeared my blood over my lips and licked them. After that, he never bothered me again.

At home, Daddy would offer up the fisherman's prayer before every meal.

"I pray that I may live to fish
Until my dying day.
And when it comes to my last cast,
I then most humbly pray:
When in the Lord's great landing net
And peacefully asleep
That in His mercy I be judged
Big enough to keep."

It was the prayer he was taught by his own Daddy. For my Grand-Daddy, it came true; he was fishing on the river with my Daddy until the day he died. Then it was Daddy's turn to lay his nets with his son, my brother, George. And so the wheel turned. They fished every incoming tide as soon as the forsythia bloomed its unhappy yellow alarm. At night I watched the lanterns they hung to mark their nets twinkle in the darkness and pretended they were the lights of the city where my shad family lived.

But know this if there is any justice in heaven for sins committed on earth, then our Lord will have one look at Daddy and throw him back. Daddy was as mean as a shad plank, nailing us with his knuckles until we felt the heat of coals on our back. My mother made excuses for him, saying his goodness was dwindling with the fish. When she was a girl, the shad run was about 400,000. Now, we were lucky if we got a fraction of that.

George inherited his cruel ways, although he never raises a hand to me. Instead, he used his words as a filleting knife. Yet I imagined myself like the shad, Daddy might have removed my scales with a blunt spoon, but it takes skill to debone a shad. I had a thousand bones, and my brother was always too clumsy to master the art. He might have owned a sharp knife, but you'll never get the sweetest meat if you don't have patience.

Mother and I made sure the fish that Daddy and George caught could be sold to Mr. Maynard for his Shad Shack. He fried them up and sold them to the travelers on Saybrook Road. We worked ten hours a day from April to May, and I could fillet over a hundred and fifty. Mother called it an art, and she'd been doing it for near on fifty years, but her fingers had gotten stiff, so she only managed half the amount she used. I tried to make up the difference, so Daddy wouldn't know, but it was hard.

Then one day, as I was running my knife over the bones from gills to tail, counting the clicks like a rosary of saints, Daddy came up behind me. I'd told Mother to take a break, and of course, Daddy saw me standing at the table alone and demanded to know where she was. I told him she felt unwell and was lying down. Daddy grabbed my wrists and dragged me against the wall. Again I had that feeling this had all happened before. Daddy's rough fingers pushed my skirt up around my waist, and he was gulping, fighting for each breath. Finally, I started to scream, and he banged my head against the wall snarling at me to be a good girl. Mother must have heard us as we'd made enough commotion to rouse Jessie. She had broken through the gate to her shed and was butting against the house.

Mother saw Daddy smack me across the face as she opened the door. Then, shouting for him to stop, she launched herself at

Daddy's back. Mother shrieked, "I will not let you beat her down the way you have me all these years, you bastard." I had never heard her raise her voice to Daddy before and indeed had never heard her swear at anything or anyone. The air seemed to leave the room, and I felt we were all underwater. Daddy moved in slow motion as he grabbed Mother by the throat, lifting her up. I watched as she started to gasp, her legs flapping wildly like the shad when they knew they were about to die. I took my boning knife and stuck it in Daddy's neck. I drew it across as if I was slicing off a keel bone.

I escaped to the river and washed my bloody fingers in the water. A mist was coming up, and I wrapped myself in its cloak of invisibility. I placed my stone heart on the river bank, unlaced my bones, and joined my breath with the fog as I let the Shad Spirit embrace me, and I left the world of men. All the men who had only ever tried to remove my spirit, ripping it away bone by bone. I knew I was home at last. So I flicked my tail joining the shoal of silvery fish flashing upstream like wishes that had just come true.

# DUCK

We walk through the slush single file, I fit my feet into his large prints, so it looks like he is walking alongside the gushing river on his own. I have always felt safest in his shadow as if nothing terrible could find me again.

When we first met after the war, so very long ago now, he told me his name, Cul, was an old family name. It seemed solid and reliable to someone who had known neither thing. Although I was named after my father, I told him I was named after Billie Holiday because my mother had loved her song 'God Bless The Child.' Then I added the half-truth, "It was the only thing she left me. She died when I was two, so I can't really remember her." My mother had loved that song, but she had left me with so much less than a blessing. I was sixteen when she died, and unfortunately, I could remember everything about her.

Now he has stopped to watch a pair of mallard ducks being swept past as if they are in a cartoon; as I join him, the clamant-capped male seems to change direction, paddling hard against the current. His dull companion sails on around the bend. Cul lets out a soft sigh and trains his ever-present camera on the ducks. I used to think that because he only ever really looked at anything through a viewfinder everything seemed smaller to him. Now I realize that is how he survived seeing all the awful things that he photographed for *Time* magazine. I reach up to touch him gently on the back of his neck. My fingers are cold, and he smiles even as he shivers, and then he pulls up the collar of his old crackly jacket and continues on. His stride increases, and I jump using his footprints as stepping-stones through the snow-shore.

Around the river's bend, we see the discarded corpses of about twenty pine trees hugging the bank, all in different stages of decomposition. The small brown duck is struggling to free herself from the branches of a tree that still had some pine needles clinging to its limbs. Cul climbs over the low stone wall and starts to move down the bank, his right foot slips into the river, I call out, but the noise of the churning water pulls away my voice, so I brush the snow from the top of the wall and sit down to wait.

After freeing the duck, Cul retrieves the flowers he has left on the wall. They look like a bright bruise against the light grey rocks and bring up all the painful pictures I always try to duck. When Cul gets to the bridge, he hesitates for a second, but I give him a slight nudge to hurry him on. He feels it like the wind hurrying him out over the water.

Taking his handkerchief out of one of the many pockets of his coat, he wipes his face. Then in a slurred tenor, he starts to sing. 'God Bless The Child.' It is difficult to hear over the tumbling river, so he sings louder as he tips the purple Lily of the Nile flowers into the water. I think I heard him say, "See you next year," as he walks away.

I watch. Every anniversary I hope he will bring our daughter; she would be fifteen now. But Cul only ever brings my favorite flowers and older and older steps. Maybe I had always been broken inside, or perhaps I had been suffering from some sort of depressive illness; all I know was I couldn't bear our daughter's crying, the constant crying. It dug a chasm through me, so I was separated from my right mind. At first, I had only pinched the white skin of my daughter, but one day, I had picked up a silver-backed hairbrush, then I knew; I was like her, my mother, and Cul would never be able to make me safe.

The river was full from the winter melt, and when I reached the bridge, I saw a pair of ducks watching me from the bank; I wrenched a smooth stone from the wall and hugged it to my chest. The ducks left as I sank under the dark surface of the water. Now, as I stand anchored to the bridge, I can see the brown duck Cul had rescued, it has been reunited with her colorful partner, and I smile at them like they are old friends. I return to my seat on the wall and, to Cul's retreating back, I whisper, "See you next year, my love. God bless."

# THE HISTORY OF CONNECTICUT'S STONE WALLS

By Robert Cooperman March 1964

## Monuments to Industry Or Piles Of Refuse?

If you have walked through any wood in Connecticut you will have seen miles of low stonewalls seemingly built without any rhyme or reason. In fact, according to the 1871 agricultural census there was 200,000 miles of stonewall throughout New England. A lot of these are old farmer's walls; they lack shape and lie in forests, sometimes miles from any obvious habitation. To understand the purpose of these walls you must first have some knowledge about the geological history of the region.

## The Stones

During the Ice Age sheets of ice covered much of North America. This glacial formation picked up stones and dragged them along in its path. This is called glacial till. When the glaciers receded the granite stones were left behind. The stones varied in size and were obstacles for settlers looking to farm the land.

## Stone Walls

The settlers had to remove the stones before they could farm the land. At first, in the late 1600s, they piled them into linear pillars at the edges of their fields using their hands or oxen. Later, a law was passed requiring farmers to fence in their animals and so the walls grew more regular and marked the boundaries of properties.

*'Before I built a wall I'd ask to know*

*What I was walling on or walling out'*

**'Mending Walls' by Robert Frost**

## Different Types Of Stone Walls

There are three types of stonewalls:

**1. Thrown Walls:** these are the most basic type of wall formed by stacking the stones in a haphazard pattern. They lack foundation and often lose stones.

**2. Laid Walls:** these walls have more structure. Due consideration was given the shape and placement of each stone. Some of the stones were shaped or 'dressed' by stonemasons and the walls took on a more formal appearance. These, however, did not allow movement of the soil beneath their foundations and so during cold weather when the water in the ground would freeze and thaw the walls were vulnerable to shift and breakage.

**3. Rubble-Filled Walls:** this third type of wall combines the best function of the other designs. They are two laid walls built alongside each other and filled with rubble in the space between the two. The outer walls hold everything together, the rubble allows the wall to settle and adjust to the forces it encounters.

*Further Reading:*
*An American Stonehenge*
*By Thomas Wentworth Higgins*

# MAYBE I GIVE A DAMN

I always thought I settled for less—for snatches. That first time when you asked if the devil looked like you, I kissed you as if I was Scarlett O'Hara. I let you think you had the wicked glint of Rhett Butler rather than the dull patina of poor old beige Ashleigh. It was the start of all my unsaid things.

We both study the decaying leaves trapped in a web outside the kitchen window. They tremble like chimes that have lost their music; a clump clustered together in the corner of the pane that trails off like people leaving a party too soon. I should take a broom to them or try to capture the brittle beauty in a photo—I do neither. You are tossing that stupid stone your brother had given you when he got back from some shoot in Appalachia. It never seemed like much of a gift to me yet you've kept it on your desk all this time.

You comment that it might be time to give the house a general spruce up. It's not much of a conversational starter, so I shrug and take my coffee outside. I sit by our pool, it's clear down the shallow end, but the deep end has a covering of dark green algae that throws up a dark shadow. I balance my cup on the wall; you had it built last year at great expense, even though you used immigrant labor, and it rings the pool like a work of art. The biscuit-colored stones fit together in a complex puzzle, unlike the low stonewall at the end of our garden. That has the appearance of a building block project undertaken by a giant child abandoned halfway through construction. But it is only meant to denote the boundary of our property, so aesthetics are not really a consideration. The other day, I was adding birdseed to the feeder by the wall, and I looked down to see something glinting in the grass. It was a heart-shaped white stone, pierced with a hole. I'm not superstitious, but I did feel a momentary shudder pass through me, so I threw it deep into the wildlife refuge beyond the wall.

I stay out there for a long time watching a tiny frog swimming laps in the pool. If you were here, you'd scoop up the tiny creature with the net and catapult it over the wall into the woods into the wild.

What does disappointment smell like? Is it the scent of another steak potpie that oozing gravy like a bloody wound that is pushed around your plate until it disintegrates into mush? I know you don't care for flaky pastry, but I serve it occasionally anyway. I play a little game to see how much of it you will eat. Tonight you surprise me; you eat the whole thing. When I look out of the window, the leaves and the web are gone.

You clear your throat and tell me you've met somebody. Somebody who has said she can't live without you, somebody so very unlike me who can barely live with you. You tell me you are no longer content to settle for less, to live your life in snatches. You speak to me as if I'm one of your patients, slowly as if what you are telling me is fair and measured. When I ask about the leaves, you look mystified.

They must have gone with the wind, I say with a laugh (or maybe it was a wail). And then I tell you I'm going for a swim. "Now?" you ask, perplexed. "I'll think about all that you've said tomorrow. Tomorrow is another day, don't you know!" I throw over my shoulder. My response sinks like a stone into your confusion.

I know it is best to get straight in; the chill takes my breath away as I make my way to the deep end. I only learned to swim when I was in my twenties, and I've never really enjoyed not being able to touch the bottom. The pool is surprisingly large, but then we have two acres of land; I try not to think about the fact we'll have to sell now. Instead, I concentrate on my breathing and the delicious heavy feeling in my arms. It seems so long since I've felt anything at all. The sun is sieved through the trees as I turn to swim back to the shallows. Then, out of nowhere, a frog jumps into my mouth.

Much later, from my seat on the wall, I see him walk to the deep end; the alga camouflages my body. But then I rise—hideously pale—and it's his turn to wail.

# BENT OVER BACKWARD

When I was little, I stood straight like other people. Sometimes, I even tipped forward like a question mark. I don't remember that; I only know because of the photos I found in the attic. When I looked at them, my younger self was upside down posed, balanced on the low stonewall that encloses our backyard or on a school stage. My mouth formed a cartoon bridge of misery. There are no images of my older self.

If I could pinpoint when it started, Jack thinks I might begin to straighten myself out, move out of my parents' house, and have a life. Yes, he used the word 'straighten,' which made me like him immediately. Jack says I needed to deal with my past so I could assert some control over my future. But, of course, he didn't use the word 'some'; he talks in absolutes, that word is mine.

Dr. Bennett ("call me Jack") is the last one in a long line of doctors. He doesn't deal in bones or genetics; he's a psychoanalyst and deals with empathy. So instead of x-rays of my skeleton, he is shining a light on my subconscious.

Jack and I rake through my childhood, but it was not in any way remarkable. I am an only child of older parents. They were a little slaphappy (still are, but I don't tell Jack that), and I tried to avoid Dad when he came home reeking of beer. That's easier now I'm grown. I helped Mom with the chores, and now I do them all. She's not an easy woman to please. She likes everything 'spick and span,' and I find it challenging to get everything done because of the extra time with Jack. Yesterday she told me I had to stop seeing

49

him; I held the heart stone that Jack had given me and for the first time, I told her 'No.' Her face was a picture, and the little white stone pulsed with heat in my hand as if to say well done.

Today Jack measured me and said I'd straightened up by three inches since starting our sessions, so maybe therapy is working. No, not 'maybe'—therapy is working.

# WHILE MEMORY HOLDS A SEAT

"There was a man who dwelt by a churchyard."

"What does dwelt mean?" Maddy asked, wrinkling her nose. "He lived by a churchyard," Nick explained, silently cursing himself for using a Shakespeare quote, but being an old English major he just couldn't help himself. "And one night each year..." Maddy interrupted again, "I don't like this story. Tell me one about Elsa." Nick had no idea who Elsa was but knew better than to ask. "This is a Christmas story." Maddy rolled her eyes dramatically, and at that moment, she looked so like her mother that Nick felt something move inside him. "Look, I'll make you a deal. If you don't tell, you can have a cookie." Maddy smiled, showing the gap in her teeth, and Nick felt another tug. She ran over to the plate gleefully and offered Nick one of the clumsily iced cookies, saying, "I made them for you, " and then she asked, "Where's your red suit?"

"I'm in disguise," Nick said. "So, on Christmas Eve, the man can leave and visit one special person and of course, that special person is you." Maddy was snaking her hand towards the plate. She knocked it, and it fell with a crash onto the stone fireplace, a fireplace that Nick had built with local stones, so long ago. The landing light came on, and Lynne's voice echoed down the stairs, "Maddy is that you? I hope you're not eating the cookies we left out for Santa?" Maddy squealed and said, "Santa said I could have one. Ask him, Mom."

Nick watched his wife enter the room. Although Nick noticed some new lines around her eyes, she was still beautiful. "Sleep now, or Santa won't come," Lynne said. Maddy yawned as she said, "But Mom, he's already here." Lynne shushed her and bent down to smooth the impression out of the chair where Nick had been sitting.

His girls were changing, and Nick knew that's how it should be. He was the only one who would never age, never be a day older than the day he lost control of the car. He'd crashed into a low stonewall and the car flipped over. Nick said, "Merry Christmas, my loves. Until next year," but all Lynne heard was a ghostly whisper of the wind in the chimney.

# THE GHOST IN MY MACHINE

Joan, a colleague of mine, told me a story she read online about an ordinary man whose dead girlfriend kept contacting him on Facebook. Through the mush and the static, she appeared sitting or standing in photos where she would've been if she weren't dead. He saw her laughing behind a mask at Halloween or the back of her head in a concert crowd.

When I was young, I believed behind the finch's song the voices of the dead were calling my name, and so it made sense to look for you in all the white noise.

I read about how the Egyptians wrote letters to their recently departed in bowls—begging for help with the insoluble problems of living. And in Mexico, they built altars—altares de Muertos—to welcome the spirits. So I ordered a set of three mini teak altars from Etsy and set up a shrine in the wardrobe so our daughter won't find it. I arranged the photo of us on a rocky beach in Malta just after uni, your lighter engraved with a bee that you nervously flicked before you asked me to marry you. I weigh down a sliver of your favorite sweater with your lucky stone that you found in Devil's Den on a camping trip when you were eight. I used to laugh each time I saw it at the bottom of the washing machine because you'd left it in a pocket. And of course, you didn't have it with you that day. Around the rim of a paper bowl, I wrote, "I'm sorry. I'm here waiting for you," and then I filled it with bright marigolds. I know if only I could talk to Dr. Bennett I might find a better way to cope but when I rang his office they told me his wife had passed away and he was on leave. We all have our ghosts.

The flowers turned brown, and I found out the dead girlfriend story was just a well-crafted spooky tale posted on Reddit. Your ghost began to shrink to a shadow in a selfie or a whisper on a windy night. Or maybe I'd lost my desire to be haunted.

I know someday, we will all be ghosts, fragments of memory on a device, and if they want to hear the voices of the dead, they'll sit around a campfire and just press play. Standing in the rain shadow now, feeling blurry at the edges, I listen to your voicemail—wavery, so you even sound like a spirit. 'Call me back when you get this.'

# SERIAL KILLERS

Joan glanced at her face in the mirror to see if all the dead bodies she had encountered had left any outward marks. Apart from the slight creases under her eyes, she still looked like the raw, green girl she was when she experienced her first murder. Looking back on the photographs from that time, she seems shiny and desirable, although she would never admit it aloud. The sense of accomplishment she got from solving that case had fixed itself like permanent make-up on her face. Her cheeks were smudged with a coral blush, and her lips bee-stung from her chewing on them like gum. She started to dress with more care, each piece of clothing selected for how others would see her, she wanted them to think 'she's in charge.' Was it any wonder she had become addicted to the Joan she became when she was weeks' deep in a new crime? Lately, though she could feel herself becoming quite blasé about death, the last corpse had barely registered, and it had been a particularly gruesome specimen.

In the last decade, Joan had lost more than one relationship through her need to be immersed in her cases. Most men couldn't cope with playing second fiddle to her preoccupation, and when she started to cancel dates, they quickly left. Pete, who had hung around longer than most, told her, "You know it's not normal. You're letting real life pass you by." As if shacking up with him in his twilight basement apartment was the sort of 'real life' everybody craved. But then, late at night, as she stared at her computer screen with tired eyes, she thought he might have been right. Recently she had been toying with the idea of calling Pete to affect reconciliation. Although she hated his apartment, she did like the way he clung to her fiercely in the night. He was like a human-weighted blanket allowing her to sleep without dreaming of victims silently screaming for justice.

This last case that Joan was involved with was an exceptionally high-profile murder case, and all the papers, both local and statewide, had picked it up. This gave her a frisson of excitement that she hadn't felt in a while. She devoured the details. It transpired that some kids had discovered a suitcase containing a dismembered head. When she first saw the hard-shelled bag, it was shrouded in early morning mist and surrounded by crouching PCs from M Division. "It looks like an inexperienced screenwriter's idea of foreshadowing," she mumbled to her new partner. He snorted and muttered, "I thought you were anti-metaphor! I just hope they're not messing up evidence!" And he went to make some coffee.

The killer turned out to be a boy just out of his teens; the victim his pimp. He'd been fed drugs and groomed for prostitution. Once he got too pitiful to attract punters, the boy was abandoned. He took revenge by cutting off the pimp's head with a machete. Her partner argued these were mitigating circumstances, that the boy deserved some sympathy. She knew then things had spiraled out of control. She felt nothing for the boy's plight; her overwhelming urge was to start binge-watching another series straight away. She picked up the remote and flicked onto Netflix. There was a trailer for a true crime series set in Connecticut. Joan vaguely remembered the case; a doctor had been accused of killing his wife by drowning her in their pool. She watched all six episodes and she knew she could not go on like this.

The following day Joan got up early. In the mirror, her face looked like an echo of herself from just a couple of weeks ago. Her cheeks had collapsed, the lines etched around her dark eyes looked as if the tines of a fork had gouged them out. She looked down at the small mound that she had cultivated with snacks and wine as she watched her latest show and realized that her addiction was impacting her health. It was time to kick the habit.

Joan canceled her cable subscription and downloaded an app, 'Walking for Weight Loss' and got herself a dog she called Poirot. A week later, she was striding along a trail in the 'Devil's Den Preserve.' When Poirot started barking and bounded over the low stonewall as if he could sense the ghosts of the sheep that would have been grazing there centuries ago. Sighing Joan climbed carefully over the wall; since she had started walking she had wondered about these walls that were strung like necklaces through the trees. As Joan got closer to Poirot she could see he was digging frantically and to her surprise he emerged with a bone in his mouth. It was much too long to belong to an animal. Joan said sternly "Bad boy. Drop" and she stepped over the bone, rolled her eyes, and pulled Poirot back over the wall to return to the path.

# COLD CASES AND CAFFEINATED KISSES

Detective Cooperman consulted his notes, cleared his throat, and said, "The forensic anthropologists report concluded the bones belonged to a female approximately 55 inches tall." At this, the Chief interrupted him, "Fifty-five?" He raised an eyebrow as he did the mental calculations. "God forbid. Are you telling me the bones belong to a child?"

Cooperman suppressed his irritation; he'd been living on coffee and doughnuts ever since the bones had been discovered behind a wall in Devil's Den four days ago, and his stomach sloshed uncomfortably as he stood up from the edge of the desk where he'd been perched.

"Um no, Sir, it appears the bones have been buried for quite some time, possibly centuries. There was evidence of perimortem trauma to the...." Again the Chief interrupted him, "Centuries, you say? Well, thank fuck for that. This case is too cold for us then Coops. Pass it on. Maybe UConn might be interested. Get in touch with their Forensic Anthropology department and, for God's sake, get some shut eye, you look worse than a corpse."

Cooperman flipped his notebook shut. He had been relieved when he'd been told the bones probably dated from colonial times. Cooperman thought it was perhaps a grave inadvertently dug up by a large animal. The only thing that gave him pause was the broken wrists and the reconstructed cranium showing blunt force trauma to the face and skull. "Poor bitch" he'd thought to himself as he poured another cup of coffee.

To his disgust, it was cold, but he drank it anyway as he turned to his screen to read the autopsy report on yet another young woman. Her head had been caved in with a blunt object, possibly a stone just like all the others before her. He shouted at Josie, the newest uniform, to make fresh coffee. She refilled the pot but didn't bring him a cup, "She's a bit of a bitch isn't she?" he said to Rogers sitting opposite him. Rogers grunted, "Young girls have no idea these days do they?'

Later, at home, Cooperman unfurled the hose and trained the stream of water at the rock he had taken out of the trunk of his car. Rivulets of rusty water ran away into his lawn. He picked up the rock, weighing it in his hand as if he was buying a melon. He had chosen this house for the wildlife refuge bordering the back yard, so secluded and peaceful. He walked towards it and placed the rock in the wall. Cooperman had started to build this wall a few years ago. It has grown in fits and starts depending on his frame of mind. As he fitted the new rock into the wall like a puzzle piece the other rocks seemed to screech out, an echo of all the other lost women, but it was probably just the wind and there was nobody to hear anyway.

# WANNABE IN MY GANG?

Mickey told me I sleep like a question mark—knees towards my stomach, toes pointing to the bottom of the bed. It was spot on because I've always felt like a question rather than a statement; a why girl, instead of a when I grow up, I want to be, kind of girl.

I'm nothing like Nancy; she wants to be a ballerina and is pirouetting relentlessly across the floor. When we first met, she seemed effervescent, a glass of prosecco; now, she's unsmiling and ragged, like a flat Diet Coke. Then there's Paula, who wants to be a librarian because that's where she feels safest, her body odor mingling with the fusty scent of the damp books stored on the basement level. At the moment, Paula's head is buried in *The Mosquito Coast*, a book I know she's read at least twice already.

Mickey gave Paula that book when she joined last year. He always wanted to be a high school teacher and is always quoting vast chunks of literature, trying to impress us. When he first met Paula, he told her, "I love how honest Thoreau is about America being mired in materialism and conformity." If he'd said that to me, I'd have rolled my eyes and moved on, but Mickey is cleverer than that.

When I mentioned to the gang that I'd never had any idea what I wanted to do with my life—Juliet, always the kindest, suggested I should go to college with her. She still wears the lanyard the college sent with her acceptance letter. It's a bit grubby because she continually worries her fingers over it like a rosary. When she said that, I nodded, even though I knew it was impossible. I've never graduated high school, and Juliet won't go now she's in the gang.

It is amazing how he knows which girls are like a guava, green and a bit prickly on the outside but ripe, pink, and looking for love on the inside. Although in my case, it's true to say, my darkness was blooming on the bush long before I met Mickey. He is only the last in a long line of men who swept me up with a promise of being the answer to all my questions.

Yesterday Mickey found a potential member, Vanessa; she has the same wide-eyed doe look and blonde hair that marks her as an obvious recruit. Juliet sat next to her as she sobbed, stroking her back in a motherly gesture, which had no effect. In fact, she started to cry harder. Finally, wiping her nose with the back of her hand, she stuttered, "I just want to gggo home." Her lipstick was smeared, and her mascara had blackened her eyes. We all knew Mickey wouldn't like that. He's always saying that women are 'the decorative sex,' so we should care about our appearance. He put his hands on his hips and said in what I think of as his teacher's voice, "Now, Vanessa, what was it you told me? How you hate your stepfather? How you couldn't live with him anymore? Get some sleep, and tomorrow I'll get us some food, and you'll feel better. McDonald's okay?" When Vanessa carried on sobbing, Mickey sighed and turned on the radio; the frothy lyrics of 'Wannabe' bubbled out. Mickey doesn't let us watch TV; he says it curdles the brain, but he does let us listen to the radio. Mickey grimaced and said, "For God's sake, I don't know what's happened to music. Is it any wonder you girls aren't safe these days? Listen to that, 'likes it in your face,' it's disgusting, that's what it is," and he turned the knob viciously until he found a channel more to his liking.

"Clean up," Mickey told Vanessa, gesturing toward the sink, "and make sure you don't touch that radio. I don't want to come back and find you've been listening to that Spice Girls trash. I'll see you tomorrow." As soon as he'd left, Vanessa tried to open the door; of course, we wanted to tell her that Mickey locked it to keep us safe, but she was beyond listening to anybody.

Someone was reading a poem about what women want on the radio. Apparently, it's a red dress, and it reminded me of the dress I wanted for Prom; it was as red as a scream. But Mom picked out a mauve dress, the color of a bruise. When I tried it on, I could feel my bones soften. The factory-made lace was as unyielding as my catholic upbringing, but at least the puffed sleeves emphasized the tininess of my waist. I liked that. Now don't think for a minute Mom was trying to make a silk purse out of a sow's ear—I was beautiful. But it was a beauty that scared her. Mom could hear my future giggling underneath that voluptuous skirt. She'd seen the men sniffing around, scenting truffles in my over-developed curves. All these years later, I can finally admit she was right to be fearful.

Of course, I wonder if she's looking for me. Maybe she's contacted the police, but even if she has, they'll tell her I have form. I've been running away from her all my life; it's only now I wish I could run back to her. When I said this to the girls, they stopped what they were doing and looked at me with a mixture of sadness and surprise. You see, I've always been the stoic one; no matter what Mickey throws at us, I just keep painting my nails red with the polish Mickey buys for us. It's called 'All I Need is You,' which I once thought was a sweet sentiment but not anymore. Even so, it's become a compulsion, but no matter how carefully I apply the polish each night, by the following day, the varnish is smudged, and my cuticles are bitten raw. And it's true, I never complain; I remove the polish and start again. I suppose I'm luckier than the others; I never had hopes for the future, just as well, really, as Mickey has made sure I will never leave him.

Juliet was talking to Vanessa as if she was one of the preschool children Juliet dreams of teaching. It's how she spoke to each newbie, telling them everything would be all right. I think she knows that's not true by now, but like Paula's chain reading or Nancy's pirouettes, she is stuck spinning the same lies over and over again.

Juliet is the oldest, and she's been with Mickey the longest, his first gang member. She likes to tell us how she met him in The Labyrinth Bar, how he charmed her by quoting Austen, "You pierce my soul. I am half agony, half hope." When she first said this, Paula snorted and replied, "*Persuasion* really? He quoted that from *Persuasion*. I'm surprised he didn't say 'When pain is over, the remembrance of it becomes a pleasure,' I think that's more like Mickey's modus operandi."

I've never told them that Mickey misquoted *The Great Gatsby* the first time he met me. "You've been drifting here and there trying to forget the sad things that happened to you, but if you stay with me, I promise no more sad things will ever happen." I told you he was clever. Did I believe him? I don't think so, but I wanted to, and that's what we gang members all have in common.

Vanessa is curled up on the stained mattress like a comma; I know she doesn't have long. Mickey will return with a double cheeseburger for him and a happy meal for her as if she were a child. He'll start by cajoling, telling her she deserves so much more than life has given her and that he will take care of her from now on. Then, he'll try to feed her French fries like a mother hen with a chick. And finally, he'll flourish an Oreo milkshake that, like a magic trick, will make her disappear.

The rest of us will watch as she lies drugged on the mattress and as Mickey takes the nail polish. He will painstakingly paint Vanessa's nails, and then read aloud from the book he's specially chosen for her as he waits for the polish to dry. Finally, he'll take a stone out of his gym bag and weigh it in his hands like a prize pumpkin. The others will look away because it's hard to watch what comes next, but I do. It's the least I can do for Vanessa, and I hope she can feel she's not alone.

And I will be the one who sits and holds her hand until she comes around. You see, when she wakes, she'll have joined our ghostly gang, and of course, she'll have lots of questions.

# MISS SPENT

I didn't set out to lead a life of crime, but then again, I didn't set out to do a lot of things. As I went into the shop, I walked past the glossy chocolate bars, and my fingers tingled like I'd held them too close to the bar heater. I was tempted to put one in my pocket, but I didn't as I was trying to be good. There was a soft, doughy belt around my middle, and I knew I still looked pregnant if I didn't hold my tummy in. Last Monday at the market, a new stallholder asked me how many months along I was. I tried to laugh as I said, "I'm not pregnant, just fat," as if it was all some big joke, but inside, I felt sick. You see, I'm not really fat; my wrists are tiny, you can see the blue veins through my skin, like a map of the A-line on the subway. And I know my legs look good in a short skirt as Mom told me I should cover them up when she caught Steve looking at them.

Anyway, I rummaged around in my over-large bag, looking for something to take away the nasty taste in my mouth that I always get whenever I think about Steve. I found a mint; it was a bit fluffy, God knows how long it'd been there, but I wiped it off and popped it into my mouth anyway. I made a point of leaving my bag unzipped, casual-like. The mint was chalky on my tongue, so I took it out and dropped it on the floor.

I sailed past the bottles of nail polish. The candy-colored shades reminded me of when my nails were like talons, but that was before Dad left. I curled my sticky fingers into my palms to

65

hide my nails as they're bitten down to the quick now. I started biting them after Steve moved in with us.

I'd reached the baby aisle, and there was a young woman with a heart-shaped face and a baby bundled around her middle looking at the pacifiers. The baby was yelling blue murder, but the woman just smiled and rubbed his back. She even smiled at me as she left and said, "Teething, you know." I wanted to shout, "No, I don't know," but of course, I didn't.

Then I pulled out my scrunchie, and my hair made a curtain around my face. I picked up a can of baby formula and weighed it carefully in my fingers like I was choosing a melon, and then I slipped it quickly into my bag. The rush was immediate, as thick and as golden as honey. The can pulsed in my bag, warming my belly, and I didn't feel numb anymore.

Of course, I knew not to leave straight away. I repeated in my head, "Linger, and browse, linger and browse" as I put my hand in my pocket looking for my lucky white stone. Dad and I found it when we were out hiking in Devil's Den. He said it looked like a heart with a hole in it. But that was before he left, before we moved to the city. And I'd forgotten I'd tucked it in her blanket when I was allowed to say goodbye.

I headed to the perfume counter. I picked up a curved hot-pink bottle; it was dotted with tiny glass chips, a bottle for Disney's idea of a princess or maybe a genie. Do you know, once upon a time, I believed in happily ever after and wishes but not anymore. Anyway, I sprayed the scent on a cardboard stick and wafted it in front of my face. I was surprised, it smelled like a clean white T-shirt, so I spritzed it all over my hoodie. I hoped it would mask the sour smell, but then I noticed a shop assistant was watching me. I put down the bottle, fighting the urge to run; my thoughts slapped me around the face. "Breathe slowly," I told myself. "Smile at the old witch giving you the stink eye as if you don't have a care in the world."

Wandering down the next aisle, I found myself amongst the greeting cards; a mountain of pale pink and blue cards shouted *Congratulations on Your New Baby*. I swallowed something hard in my throat and moved along. The cards, further ahead, were printed with shiny woodland animals, sparkly fish, and glittering insects. Of course, the only bugs or animals you got around here were anything but pretty, but I suppose nobody would buy a card with a cockroach or a rat on it. I felt like I was walking through a paper meadow far away, one full of flowers and magical creatures, and I smiled for the first time in a long time.

I chose one with a butterfly and a rose and thought about slipping it into my bag so I could send my smile to her. But I didn't know where they'd taken her, so I put the card back and turned to leave the shop. "Excuse me, Miss," a razor-sharp voice pursued me.

Later, when the police found out I didn't even have a baby anymore, I could see the pity in the eyes of the female police officer. She told me her name was Josie and that she could put me in touch with people who could help me. And all I could do was shrug as if I didn't care. But of course, I did.

# WALLED-IN

The photo on your nightstand shows our summer-damp daughter clasping a frog in a jar. You are there too, slightly out of focus, squinting at the water. I remember her shaking off droplets and tipping happy bubbles down her throat. Bea dragged you away from the horizon to look for bugs in our ivy-clad tumbling stonewall. Even when she was little, she could feel you wanted to be somewhere else. It was always me that rubbed ointment into her sunburnt shoulders after the bath. When she cried and asked where you were, I told her you were dancing with fireflies. And sometimes you were—but mostly you disappeared beyond the wall and were gone all night.

That Christmas, I took the peeled twigs, the stones I had polished, the bird feathers, and photos we gathered of that summertime and wove them into a wreath to celebrate our family. If only I had known a wreath represented the crown of thorns, I would never have mangled our keepsakes with the holly.

We lived in Connecticut, in a white-clapboard house with black shutters like false eyelashes. It had a plaque that proclaimed it was 'Captain David Cooperman's House 1789' and a rubble-filled wall ringing the property that looked like it hadn't been touched since that time. I remember you printing pink hearts on doilies and hanging them in the kitchen one soggy February afternoon. After, you made jam tarts with Bea, insisting that she hide them around the house so the Knave of Hearts could not steal them. The following day I trod on a forgotten tart in the dark of the coat cupboard when I was getting my raincoat and cursed. You were watching me through the beveled window that was set into the wall between us. You flounced past me out of the front door into the rain without a coat. Although Bea was older, she still cried after you, hoping to reel you back. That time you were gone for a week, and I spent seven dusty days searching for secrets in the attic. Finally, I found a silver-toned photograph of your father leaning on the rail of a boat. I had never met him as he had left when you were small.

Once Bea had gone, I knocked down our house and built it back with tiny windows and doors. I rebuilt the thrown wall, not realizing without foundation, it would continue to lose its stability, throwing down boulders like broken promises. Later, I added fences to stop the deer from eating our strawberries. I was only hoping to stop the drafts and make our garden an oasis, but you thought I had done it to stop you from leaving. You screamed—I was walling you in. Whenever I asked you what I could do to make you happy, you never would tell me. Rather, you would talk in a stream, words hopping like frogs, and I could only ever capture the odd one—space—solitude—kindness. And sometimes, your yells would burst the dry air, and the words soaked everything. It was only much later I found the blooms of black mold, not knowing the spores had already settled in your lungs. But that is all blood under the bridge now.

In my desperation, I took a job on an island ruled over by a mythical Merlion to persuade you there might still be magic for us to find in the world. When we were younger, the gutters of New London were lined with gold—glistening leaves—so we knew it was fall. Here we only see the seasons change as you make your own place settings for each holiday, just like your mother does. She never really accepted two women could live together and raise a family. She mellowed after we adopted Bea and she insists we stay in her house every holiday time. I would lie next to you in your old room with Bea on a blow-up mattress and feel full up.

Last November, you balanced plastic pumpkins to create a tiered stand for chocolate leaves, artfully arranged, so they looked like a drift of dirty tears. In this Garden City, you waited in line for an hour with all the other ex-pats to buy a turkey from a butcher transplanted to Singapore from New Zealand. You were happy when you returned, but we left the bird in the oven too long, as we couldn't remember what we were thankful for. The next day you started to cough.

Steadily, you got weaker and weaker; eventually, the doctors told me there was nothing to do as you refused chemo. You said to me that you did not want your last days to be poisoned, too. I would sit by your bed teaching myself how to knit from YouTube so I could make 'Socks for Soldiers,' a pasttime from another era. My clicking needles lulled like a mantra and added life to our little space. Now even that is gone. Next to the photo is a snow globe that you bought for yourself. When I asked you why, you told me it was to remind you that once you knew snow. I pick it up, shake it and realize I have grown old, leading you unwillingly by the hand and resenting what is not there in you. If only I had seen you like a snowflake whose beauty is made up of the spaces that are not filled.

I find the wreath and take it apart. I choose the stone we found in Bea's blanket that first night with her, and press it into your palm. It is shaped like a heart with a hole at its center, you smile, and I know my heart will never close the hole you leave behind.

# BIRD BRAINED

I was seventy when the bird flew into my ear and settled in the cage of my chest. I had been out in the garden berating Jorge, the man I was paying to rebuild my garden wall. Of course I wasn't doing it out loud—out loud I was smiling and telling him it was not a problem that he was late again. I turned to go inside, when a colorful bird swept past me and I felt a fluttering in my ear. At first I thought I was imagining it, I often felt I was on a roundabout like the rusty playground wheel of my childhood but knew it was due to ear crystals that sent mixed messages to my brain. I assumed this weird sensation was probably the next manifestation of aging.

I made coffee and took out a mug and my lemon cookies to Jorge. As I rested them on one of the boulders it felt warm to the touch. The wind was starting to gust and I watched with trepidation as one of the tilted trees waved like a demented baseball umpire. Then I heard bird song, high-pitched and repetitive, echoing in my breast. Panicking that I was about to have a heart attack I hurried inside to phone my doctor's emergency appointment number. A receptionist with a blunt manner asked me what was wrong. "This morning I heard…well….tweeting? In my chest?" I said, hating the stammer in my voice. The receptionist sighed, "Any pain? Swelling in your legs? Breathlessness? A cough?" When I answered "No," she said, I didn't need to go to the emergency room but I should come to see the doctor.

Over the next few days, I had various tests, but according to the specialist my heart was remarkably healthy for 'a woman of my age.' I could tell that he thought I might need another sort of doctor when he questioned me about any recent life changes. I mentioned my daughter had moved to Singapore and that she'd died a few years ago from lung cancer. And then when I said my Frank had passed three months ago, so I was on my own for the first time in fifty years, he nodded like one of those dogs you get for a car dash. "Grief can do funny things. Have you considered counseling?" he continued to drone on but the bird's singing distracted me. It had stopped tweeting and was now belting out 'Knees Up Mother Brown,' a song that my Nana used to sing to me; such a happy memories of my childhood and I only just stopped myself from joining in. I left the hospital with a fan of leaflets and a smile.

My mother was what was called 'flighty'; she didn't land for too long in any one place. I never knew my father; he died in an accident at work when I was a baby. She spent my childhood hopping from one town to another following unreliable men or angry men or men who never wanted a ready-made family. She had left me with her grandmother and she would swoop in unexpectedly, arms full of presents suitable for a much younger child and promise this time she was staying. But soon the next bright thing would catch her eye and she would be off , telling me once she was set up she would send for me but she never did.

My Nana was a stern woman; she dressed in floral aprons and always wore her hair up in a cotton candy confection that she lacquered into a helmet so the scent of hairspray surrounded her like a halo. She liked to hand out discipline with a wooden spoon and the adage 'Spare the rod, spoil the child.' But Nana had loved music hall in her youth back in England and she taught me all the songs she remembered. On a Saturday night we would put on a show for an invisible audience and then something magical happened, my unsmiling Nana would shed her wrinkles and transform, her voice smoky from her forty-a-day habit she would sing her heart out.

Now listening to the bird in my heart I was back at her kitchen table watching her empty the filter from her cigarette holder, the black treacle-like tar wiped on a tissue like the devil's snot. She had started smoking when she arrived in the US. Then both things had the ring of glamor for her. Later when I was in my twenties and she was closing in on eighty I tried to get her to stop. She laughed and said, "Something's going to get me, but it won't be this." And she was right; she had a heart attack and passed away in her sleep.

Back home I filed the leaflets in the trash. Outside the weather was getting progressively worse. Through the window I could see the wind was blowing rain in horizontal threads and the stones littered the lawn like disembodied heads. As I turned away the bird was singing 'Champagne Charlie is my name." Opening the fridge, there were two bottles of Veuve Clicquot lying side by side like a couple of pot-bellied sunbathers. Frank and I had been saving them, but for what I couldn't remember. Grabbing one by the smooth foil I sang along with the bird and I popped the cork.

I woke up realizing I had wet the bed, throwing me into a prickly panic; my arm tingled where Nana had hit me with the wooden spoon yesterday. There was a bird, its black and white throat trembling as it screeched and pecked at the buttons on the phone, and I heard Nana shout, "Stop screaming. I'll have your guts for garters if you've wet the bed again." Somewhere I thought I heard high-pitched bird song or maybe it was a siren.

# NEW MESSAGE

To:Holeintheheadreview@gmail.com

Cc/Bcc, from JorgeSalvadar@gmail.com

Subject: Submission Poetry

Dear Editor,

Please consider my poem Caravanning in Trump's America.

As requested a short bio:

Jorge Salvadar is a builder of walls and a poet who aims to take walls down. He was born in Oaxaca, Mexico and he now lives in Connecticut. His work mainly deals with his experiences of being an immigrant in America. He has been published by Tofu Arts Press, Green Ink Poetry, Bee House Journal, and has upcoming work in Every Day Fiction.

**Caravanning In Trump's America**

I follow
The crazy paving of my thoughts
Building a new road

Through the court of the oval moon
Away from the wayfarers
Whirring through a grand tour of Meridia
I can no longer stomach their tales
Beaten smooth to soften a sullen heart
I walk on into the unkind orange and blue
Doddering up to a gleaming city
Reimagined crowning a desert dune
Here the Sandman bids me slumber
He unlaces my work boots
And veils my night terrors
So my flight of fancy
Glossy shines like a crystal note
From a wondrous Bel-Canto
It rocks me to clover sleep
And splendid creatures
Windmill around to keep me safe

But this American dreaming cannot last
My face uncovered sees
The Prince of Stories
Ride hard away
Spilling the blood warm offerings
Left to sluice my journey
And I am left with only dust

In my outstretched hands
I try to show him
The precious drops
Of what might have been
But he is behind his wall
And I cannot climb up
With my forbidden load

Thank you in advance for your kind consideration.

Regards,
 Jorge Salvadar

# LOVE SHACK MAINTENANCE

I start to type up the final questions for the mid-term exam for the poetry course I teach on the 'Moshup Poets.' It is by my favorite poet; Tom Rutherford and I always throw it in as a relief from the style and tone of the other poets that make up the canon. Personally I think most of the members were trying to be too clever for their own good, especially John Trumbell. He is the most famous member of the group and 'Becoming an Unbeliever' is probably the best know poem, but I have always found his language oppressive. Although of course, he did call for the abolition of slavery and full education rights for women—I have to give him that.

Rutherford only wrote a clutch of poems, as he died young. The Stone Heart was the last one he wrote when he was working on his father's farm. I love the last verse, although the last lines have always been a puzzle. It always provokes discussion—how Rutherford moves from such a personal account of his life to encompassing the evils of colonialism. And, the imagery of a patchwork-quilted land is the perfect way to describe Connecticut.

*My heart is a notched stone*

*And the lowing woods cry out*

*But the soon-vanishing men do not hear*

*They are building a monument that only God will see*

*Long grey lines in seams like a patchwork quilt*

*Yet they only bring cold comfort to the land*

*As they were created to smother*

*The ones that slept here*

*Those that did not dream of Utopia*

Beautiful and so lyrical, it makes me think of last weekend.

Luke and I had driven out trying to fill the day. We played the old game of taking turns to call out directions at each four-way stop. These days I felt we have less and less to tell each other, so I thought getting lost together might divert us from how lost we are at home.

Luke had spotted a field of gold grass—he insisted it was calling out to him for the picnic. I suspected it was just because he needed to pee. He is always trying to make ruin romantic. I pointed out the sky probably threatened rain, but Luke supposed if the heavens opened, we could take refuge on the porch of the abandoned shack next door. So we parked and walked back through snags and tangles—who forgot to pack the cork-screw— why couldn't I remember he disliked egg salad—rhubarb, rhubarb, rhubarb.

The shack was slumped over, exhausted by its long life but still standing in spite of expectations. The striped red and green of the roof made me think of a fairground for some reason—maybe the color of a helter-skelter?

I tripped over what looked like a rabbit hole, and Luke took my hand, pulling me back. My stomach dropped as if I was falling again. Later we unrolled the ugly orange blanket; it was stained and threadbare in patches, but it was a wedding present from my mother, and it still did the job. Unpacking the cold box, I remembered it being full of special things, but after all this time, when I took them out, I saw, in the end, they were simple. Luke told me he was going to open the wine by wrapping the bottle in my sweater and smacking it on the wall of the shack. We both looked in the direction of the shack, and we both laughed.

Through the window now, I can see my neighbor leaving the house. I knock on the window and wave; I haven't seen Maggie in person for months. Luke and I had gone to the Zoom service for Garrett's funeral, but we both agreed it was no substitute for attending church to say goodbye. Even now, I still expect to see Garrett bent over like a question mark, tending his lawn.

Sighing, I return to the screen, I type the last question on the 'The Stone Heart.' 'What was Rutherford's idea of 'Utopia'? Is it the same for every individual? Discuss.' And then, I decided to ring my Mom to tell her I'd patched things up with Luke after all.

# MAKING PEACE WITH DANDELIONS

Leaving the house after so long, I walk past the two huge boulders that stand like disapproving sentinels. I can't shake the feeling I have forgotten something. I rummage through my bag, but all the important things are there—purse, keys, spare mask. Good to go then.

As I start the car, the low fuel light comes on, and then the low tire pressure light, alternating in flashing neon, like the start of a migraine. I realize I will have to sort it out now, and this starts the tears again. The radio is tuned to Garrett's favorite station, the BBC World Service; a deep voice speaks over my whimpering, "A song can make you an alcoholic or a revolutionary." This is so preposterous I let out a bark of laughter, and I'm shocked by the sound.

I change channels. A bright female voice says, "Dandelions get a bad press. In fact, they are spectacular. Their petals—a lion's mane roaring, magically turning into fairy wings as..." A man with clipped tones interrupts her, "Very poetic, I'm sure, but they do ruin your lawn." And immediately he is back from the dead—fighting the dandelions, spraying poison like a demented monk sprinkling holy water. I tried to get him to be more environmentally friendly, mixing up a solution of water and vinegar. It proved ineffective, and it left behind a lingering smell of disappointment that, with all his chemicals, he couldn't banish. Looking over at the grass now, I know he would be proud—it is a green carpet, lush, and oh so dull. Garrett had attended a class at Wilton Parks and Rec and learned how to build a stone wall. It took him months, carefully placing each stone and searching for the perfect match. Now, Garrett's hand-built wall borders his lawn, each stone like a face in an admiring gallery.

For the last forty years, I have never gone anywhere without my hand in his. But thinking about it now, his fingers were always as cold as stone in mine, dampening me down. I feel skittish like a horse without a bridle as I get out of the car and walk over to the verge. I select a giant dandelion clock and wish as I blow away the tiny, white parachute seeds over the wall. They dance like the blessing of a new beginning before settling all over the perfect lawn.

# JOSEPHINE'S CONSTITUTIONAL

Beneath a sluiced sky as empty as I try to keep my mind, the insects find me. They treat my body like a cheap hotel buffet, gorging themselves on my blood yet always managing a bite more. I feel them tickling my cheeks like John, a long-ago lover. Now I come to think of it, he liked to bite me too, and that was how Bob discovered...yes well....empty mind gathers no regrets.

I select the podcast Luke, my son-in-law, recommended. It's about people who transform winter into spring or create fake forests for film sets, and it will give me something to talk about when my daughter and Luke Facetime me on Sunday.

The podcast is actually quite fascinating. Who knew there was even such a job? Well, obviously, the people involved in the industry, I suppose. I make a mental note to tell my old neighbor, Maggie, about it. She's moved to a condo in Florida but we still talk regularly through the beauty of WhatsApp. Maggie loves her new home especially the fact she has no lawn maintenance anymore. I envy her that.

One man from New York speaks about sticking hundreds of fake leaves onto a tree's bare branches in the middle of winter, so it looked like fall. As he deadened the 'a' in fall, I am struck again by how Americans are always so literal. Why call a season autumn when you can call it Fall, so it's not just a name but also a description? Genius really. We moved from London to Connecticut with Bob's job in the year 2000, hoping for a fresh start. It's hard to imagine I've been living here for thirty years. Our three kids picked up an American twang straight away but of course Bob and I were both too old to learn new tricks.

On the podcast a girl talks about how she had to uproot a magnificent oak tree for a Nicole Kidman movie. It was two miles from where they were shooting, so she organized it to be put on a barge and sailed to the set, and then she bolted it onto a concrete slab so Nicole could climb it. And I think what an utterly awful thing to do just as I step on a spider, squishing her flat. As I look down I see a curiously shaped stone, it is like a stubby piece of chalk conspicuous against the black mud. I pick it up and put it in my pocket.

I take a seat on a wall and pour my milky tea as I read the leaflet I picked up at the beginning of the trail. Apparently it was written in 1964 and it doesn't seem to have been updated since. But at least it tells me something about the strange patchwork of low stonewalls that are strung like abandoned necklaces through the forested trails.

The government took advantage of the lack of cars on the road and repainted all the double yellow lines on my road and they left images on my retinas like the start of a migraine. So now, months into another lockdown, I'm venturing further afield. My small town has a surprising number of trails that wind through trees like a scene from a fairytale, the ones that usually involve the possibility of someone being eaten.

The sun has snuck through the branches, and I put my hand on the wall, the heat pulses, warming my palm. I take the stone out of my pocket, there is a hole in the middle of it and I fit my pinky finger in there, wearing it like a ring. Then I hear noise in the undergrowth. It rumbles like an unseen plane, but I know it's probably just the frogs mating madly. I finish my tea and put the white stone in my pocket. Then I hear a cry. Looking up, a weathered, shirtless man is striding towards me, "Hey you, yes you," he shouts as he gets closer, "What do you think you are doing?" I'm a little confused, "Um, I'm sorry," I stammer, "I thought this was a public trail. If I've trespassed, I'm sorry." The man walks right past me, and I smell sweat and something else that reminds me a little of egg salad. He picks up a stone with a pointed end and fits it like a jigsaw piece into the top of the wall. The veins of his hand stand out like those on the underside of a leaf, as he smooths it along the stone. Then he leaps over the wall and dissolves in the shadows thrown by the trees.

I walk over to the stone; it is splotched with purple moss and coiled in a crack I see a yellowed paper. When I fish it out, the stone topples and lands on my foot. The pain is indescribable, and I know I've broken a toe. I sit down, feeling nauseous. Bloody typical I think and of course the man is nowhere to be seen. I wonder if I'll be able to make it back to the car park or if I should ring someone to come and help me. My head is heavy, and I lower it between my knees for a second before I decide what to do. I felt sure I had put the white stone back in my pocket but it's there between my feet. I look at the words on the paper but they are too smudged for me to make out anything much apart from the very first words, 'My heart is a notched stone.' The paper flutters away as my fists harden, my heart drops, and I realize I am wailing, but only the other stones can hear me.

# THE MUSIC THAT REMAINS

At the edge of the day, at the end of the world, I sat wondering if I should put together a grief basket. The streets were filled with the milky tears of mothers and men pretending to be God, like a setting for a musical. Words and trumpet music by all the fallen angels.

In the light from the bloody moon, I made a cross with hair clips on the nightstand. The littlest I could do, hunkered down in my Connecticut colonial, was sign my name over and over again—an act of repentance for not paying attention sooner.

Now, many years later, I use the clips to keep my over-long hair out of my eyes and hike to an ancient place. I wonder what the hidden, tender area behind my ear is called as I pick up other people's masks; they used to be strewn about like questions, and I placed them on the low stone walls that mark the land like wrinkles.

About five years ago, I found a child's mask abandoned on the trail. It was printed with a cartoon face of a cat, tiny pink tongue, whiskers as straight and black as burnt matches. At first, it made me smile, but then hit me like a stone, I hadn't seen a child for years, not since Percy and his daughter left to go south in the hope of a kinder climate. She must be about seventeen now, if she is still alive. I look at the wall, the paper masks have dissolved, and the ties have curled up like worms after rain on the dirt below. The ones made of cotton still hang on, bleached and fluffy as if they are returning to their original state, but the synthetic ones remain unchanged. I have put a white heart-shaped stone on top of the masks; it nestles like an egg amongst the snags and tangles.

When we had to start rationing food, I turned to this wood, and it has been a saving grace for me. I have foraged nettles and berries here, trapped beavers and squirrels, but maybe more importantly, it made me realize how little I had listened before. The crickets and cicadas shake songs out of their bodies in the spring and summer, and the earth hums. In the dark, the katydids call playground taunts to me, "Katy did; she didn't; she did," and the frogs vibrate in a memory of planes. I measure my steps by seasons along a shrunken horizon and appreciate my smallness as a part of this land.

I have laid claim to a grove of maple trees, and I've taught myself how to tap them from a book I found in the abandoned library. At the tail end of winter, I hang buckets to catch all the sap and make a wood fire using a flint someone's Daddy had from Boy Scouting days. All the matches are long gone. Picking up the buckets that first time, I felt my back would break, but now I carry two at a time. I fill the pans to boil it down, and wait for it to reach the proper density, I filter out the sugar-sand through wool into canning jars, all these things I did not know before. Finally, I take it home with heavy steps to share with my clan.

After the mutation took more and more people, only a handful of us were left, somehow immune, and we had to band together and pool our resources in an attempt to survive. Once these people and I were only neighbors, we would grin at each other over our white picket fences, put out candy for trick or treating for the kids, and have a celebratory drink at Christmas. In this new world, we have burnt the fences for heat, and we have become a ramshackle extended family, both a trick and a treat of sorts. We would talk about how lucky we were to be living in a small hamlet in Connecticut where there were farms and a horse rescue center on our doorstep. Abandoning our brittle colonial homes, we have set up camp around a stone fire pit. We dragged the stones from one of the walls in the woods. Those of us who could let go of The Before have been able to scratch a living here, and sometimes we even laugh over some homebrew.

Soon it will be time to celebrate the New Year, not on the frigid last night of December but on the vernal equinox when the greenness of new growth is a worthy time to celebrate. This year, we will have a double celebration, a naming ceremony for our newest clan member, the first baby to be born in our camp.

I remember when snow made people laugh and sing soppy songs about its magic, but we know there is no poetry in snow anymore. So tonight, I will come out and pour some of my syrup as a sacrament over the last snow; and call it ice cream. I will share it with the others as we sit by the fire warming our feet on the stones. In the end, the small things have saved me, slurping sweetness under an ocean of stars, heat trapped in a stone, and listening to the song of the cicadas. Someone will fetch 'The Moshup Poets' Collected Works,' and we will take it in turns to read our favorites out loud. I will read Rutherford's "Ode to Yellowing" and marvel again that a man who lived centuries before me could so capture my heart and stop it turning to stone.

Under the canopy of the grizzled trees we bend like saplings towards each other. My heartbeat is loud like someone stamping their boots on stone steps; the cicadas are making music in the trees and my restless mind stills.

# ABOUT THE AUTHOR

Adele Evershed was born in Wales and has lived in Hong Kong and Singapore before settling in Connecticut. Her prose and poetry have been widely published. She has been nominated for the best of the net for poetry and the Pushcart prize for poetry and short fiction. *Finishing Line Press* published Adele's first poetry chapbook, *Turbulence in Small Places*. Her novella-in-flash, *Wannabe*, was published by *Alien Buddha Press* in May. Her second poetry collection, *The Brink of Silence* is available from *Bottlecap Press*.

# ABOUT THE PRESS

Unsolicited Press is based out of Portland, Oregon and focuses on the works of the unsung and underrepresented. As a womxn–owned, all–volunteer small publisher that doesn't worry about profits as much as championing exceptional literature, we have the privilege of partnering with authors skirting the fringes of the lit world. We've worked with emerging and award–winning authors such as Savannah Cooper, Amy Shimshon–Santo, Brook Bhagat, Elisa Carlsen, and Rosalia Scalia.

Learn more at Unsolicitedpress.com. Find us on Twitter and Instagram at @UnsolicitedP.

www.ingramcontent.com/pod-product-compliance
Lightning Source LLC
Chambersburg PA
CBHW030505130626
46549CB00007B/2861